Apron
Wisdom

Apron Wisdom

A spoonful of mother's sayings

Compiled by
Georgina Harris

CICO BOOKS
LONDON NEW YORK

Dedication
TDNW

Published in 2009 by CICO Books
An imprint of
Ryland Peters & Small
20–21 Jockey's Fields   519 Broadway, 5th Floor
London WC1R 4BW   New York, NY 10012

10 9 8 7 6 5 4 3 2 1

Design and illustrations © CICO Books 2009

A CIP catalog record for this book is available from the Library of Congress
and the British Library.

ISBN-13: 978 1 906525 50 7

Printed in China

Design: David Fordham
Illustrations: Trina Dalziel and Jane Smith
Cover illustration: Trina Dalziel

CONTENTS

Introduction

For centuries, women have maintained "There's no place like home." But the modern mom, clutching a briefcase under one arm and a rampaging toddler beneath the other, may not feel quite the same way.

Sure, society's biggest cliché is true—for a family, there simply is nothing like the warm comfort of a spotless kitchen, with pans bubbling temptingly, or the delicious calm of a cozy bed at night. A true mom also knows that the most important part of a home is the love and time the family spends together in it.

Mom instinctively understands that reading the same story nightly for months then "just one more time"—with impressions—counts more than a three-course dinner. Or that five minutes dancing round the TV to a theme tune with the kids matters more than clearing the dust off the DVD player… but what if you and the kids deserve a great home and the time to enjoy it? Can you have both?

This collection of wisdom from generations of wise women—and some men—shows you that the perfect home for you and the family is within reach—without much effort or time. *Apron Wisdom* is a collection of housekeeping secrets and inspirations,

gathered from old scrapbooks, historic manuals, and family tales, to inspire you and save you time to create the place you and your family can truly cherish.

Along with a selection of wise, witty and inspirational quotes that define and pay tribute to the most-loved people in the world, good mothers, *Apron Wisdom* includes guides to essential practicalities such as foolproof family recipes, tips on dealing with disasters, and the art of homemaking—in seconds. And along with the many wise mothers featured here, who also did the hardest job in the world, use these tributes to inspire you and to help you take a little time out—for yourself.

7

"If at first you don't succeed,
just do it like your mother
told you."

ANONYMOUS

Chapter 1

HOME IS WHERE THE HEART IS

"Laughter is brightest
in the place where
the food is."

IRISH PROVERB

"The best way to keep children home is

to make the home atmosphere pleasant

—and let the air out of the tires."

DOROTHY PARKER (1893–1967)

"There is a magic in that little world, home; it is a mystic circle that surrounds comforts and virtues never known beyond its hallowed limits."

ROBERT SOUTHEY (1774–1843)

"Home is home, be it ever so humble."

AMERICAN PROVERB

"There is nothing like staying at home for real comfort."

JANE AUSTEN (1775–1817)

"A place for everything and everything in its place."

MRS BEETON (1836–1865)

"Every day is a journey, and the journey itself is home."

MATSUO BASHO
(1644–1694)

Household Wisdom

1. A bowl of pasta and a smile is way better than six courses and a scowl.

2. Most household items can be cleaned with lemon, vinegar, or washing soda, which is both thrifty and eco-friendly.

3. Unless you want to, never cook anything that takes longer to eat than it does to prepare.

4. Cooking and housework burn approximately 200 calories an hour.

5. Women who got rich writing housekeeping books used the cash to, er, hire servants. Don't beat yourself up.

Recipe:
The Perfect Simple Cookie

Ideal for unexpected guests or a family treat at weekends.

1 cup (100g) all-purpose (plain) flour

1 cup (115g) chopped walnuts

¼ pound (110g) unsalted butter

2 tablespoons brown sugar

1 teaspoon vanilla essence

powdered sugar for dusting

Preheat oven to 350°F/180°C/Gas Mark 4. Mix the ingredients, roll into teaspoon-sized balls, and place on a buttered baking sheet. Bake for 15 minutes. When cool, dust with powdered sugar, and serve.

"I have been very happy with my homes, but homes really are no more than the people who live in them."

NANCY REAGAN (1921–)

"A house is made of walls and beams; a home is built with love and dreams."

ANONYMOUS

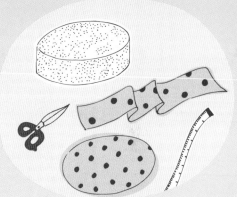

"Home isn't where our house is, but wherever we are understood."

CHRISTIAN MORGENSTERN (1871–1914)

"I hate housework! You make the beds, you do the dishes—and six months later you have to start all over again."

JOAN RIVERS (1933–)

"Cooking is like love.
It should be entered into
with abandon or not
at all!"

HARRIET VAN HORNE
(1920–1998)

Chapter 2

THE FOOD
OF
LOVE

"Stressed? Spell it backwards for the cure."

THE WICKS AND
WHITNEY LADIES'
ADVICE SERVICE,
LONDON

"A mother is a person who, seeing there are only four pieces of pie for five people, promptly announces she never did care for pie."

ANONYMOUS

"Tell me what you eat, and I will tell you what you are."

JEAN ANTHELME BRILLAT-SAVARIN (1755–1826)

"Burnt food is the perfect excuse
for a visit to a new restaurant."

ANONYMOUS

"I don't like turkey, but I do like the bread he ate."

The cardinal points of good tea-making:

- Fresh water freshly boiled, and used as soon as it boils.
- A nicely heated teapot.
- Tea poured out before it has "drawn" long enough to get the least bit bitter.

The cardinal points in good coffee-making:

- Water to be used as soon as it boils.
- Use plenty of coffee and let it stand for seven minutes.
- Use every precaution to serve the coffee piping hot.

AGNES M. MIALL, *THE BACHELOR GIRL'S GUIDE TO EVERYTHING* (1916)

Recipe:
Chocolate Mousse

Perfect for dinner à deux—and makes enough to enjoy the next day.

Gather together the same weight—8 ounces (225g) —of 70 percent dark chocolate and heavy (double) cream. Melt very, very slowly in a pan. Pour into ramekins and chill. Say no more.

"Worries go down better with soup"

"Mother: the most beautiful word on the lips of mankind"

KAHLIL GIBRAN (1883–1931)

Chapter 3

SPECIAL THINGS ABOUT BEING A MOTHER

"I think my life began with waking up and loving my mother's face."

GEORGE ELIOT (1819–1880)

"I want my children to have all the things I couldn't afford. Then I want to move in with them."

PHYLLIS DILLER (1917–)

"A man loves his sweetheart the most, his wife the best, but his mother the longest."

IRISH PROVERB

"God could not
be everywhere,
so He created
mothers."

JEWISH PROVERB

"Even as First Lady, my number one job is still to be Mom."

MICHELLE OBAMA (1964–)

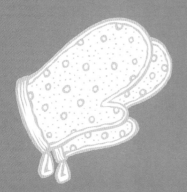

"Motherhood:
All love begins and
ends there."

ROBERT BROWNING (1812–1889)

"There is only one pretty child in the world, and every mother has it."

ANONYMOUS

"All that
I am, or
hope to be,
I owe to
my angel
mother."

ABRAHAM LINCOLN
(1809–1865)

41

Recipes:

Cheese Buttons

Reminiscent of 1950s housewifery at its finest, these cheese buttons take moments but look impressive.

1¾ cups (175g) all-purpose (plain) flour, with an extra pinch for rolling

12 tablespoons (200g) butter at room temperature

4 cups (500g) grated Emmental cheese

1 teaspoon grainy French mustard

Preheat oven to 300°F/150°C/Gas Mark 2. Blend the ingredients in a food processor. Roll the dough into a tune and cut slices ⅛ inch to ¼ inch (about 5mm) thick. Make four "buttonholes" in each slice. Bake on ungreased baking sheets for 20–25 minutes, and serve warm.

Pears on Pears

A dinner-party dish that caters to everyone. Serves 4.

2 ripe avocado pears

2 ripe pears

Bunch of tarragon

Vinaigrette

Peel and slice the pears and lay in fans on each plate. Drizzle with vinaigrette. Just before serving, tear up tarragon and sprinkle each dish with the torn leaves.

Emergency Etiquette for Entertaining

1. For emergencies—i.e. unannounced guests: Spray furniture polish onto a radiator to give the impression you've spent hours cleaning. Then only turn on side lights.

2. A jug of roses on a table improves the taste of food no end.

3. Stick to two main colors when decorating the table—say, blues and whites for fresh girly lunches, reds and violets for a full-on dinner.

4. If you are not a confident cook, invest in large wine glasses.

5. Always spend as much time choosing soft drinks—elderflower cordial or fresh juices—as you do picking the wine.

"The heart of a mother is a deep abyss at the bottom of which you will always find forgiveness."

HONORÉ DE BALZAC
(1799–1850)

"If I had a flower for each time I thought of my Mother, I could walk in my garden forever."

ANONYMOUS

"The patience of a mother might be likened to a tube of toothpaste —it's never quite all gone."

"A mother understands
what a
child does not say."

JEWISH PROVERB

Chapter 4

MORE WORDS
OF
INSPIRATION

"The moment a child is born, the mother is also born. She never existed before. The woman existed, but the mother, never. A mother is something absolutely new."

OSHO (1931–1990)

"The doctors told me that I would never walk, but my mother told me I would, so I believed my mother."

WILMA RUDOLPH, AMERICAN ATHLETE (1940–1994)

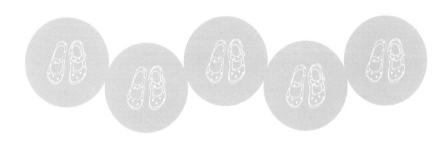

"The law of love could be best understood and learned through little children."

MAHATMA GANDHI (1869–1948)

"I remember my mother's prayers and they have always followed me. They have clung to me all my life."

ABRAHAM LINCOLN (1809–1865)

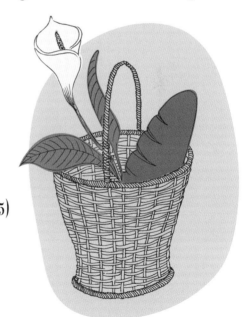

"After my mother,
I never needed
anyone else."

MAE WEST (1893–1980)

"A mother is the truest friend we have, when trials, heavy and sudden, fall upon us; when adversity takes the place of prosperity; when friends, who rejoice with us in our sunshine, desert us when trouble thickens around us; still will she cling to us, and endeavor by her kind precepts and counsels to dissipate the clouds of darkness, and cause peace to return to our hearts."

WASHINGTON IRVING (1783–1859)

10-Second Tips That Last for Days

1. Sprinkle linen water or your favorite perfume on to drying bed linen.

2. Bleach white linen with oxygen sachets from the supermarket for a crisp, snowy bedtime that lasts.

3. Put half a lemon in an empty dishwasher to refresh it.

4. Change kitchen sponges, cloths, and wooden spoons more often than you think—sparkling cloths and tools are the first thing to catch the eye.

5. Put two tablespoons of washing soda in the wash compartment to get rid of marks.

Deal with Domestic Disasters

1. Get rid of heat marks and drink rings
by rubbing in a dab of butter on the stain
and leaving it overnight.

2. Revive crushed spots of carpets and rugs by
popping an ice cube over them and watching
it melt.

3. Clean stains from wallpaper by rubbing them with a slice of
fresh white bread.

4. Clean up broken glass with a burger bap—it will pick up
the shards.

5. To put the oven out if it catches fire: cover the area with salt.

"Behave in life as you would at a banquet. As something is being passed around, it comes to you; stretch out your hand, take a portion of it politely. It passes on; do not detain it. Or it has not come to you yet; do not project your desire to meet it, but wait until it comes in front of you."

EPICTETUS (55–135)

"One generation plants the trees, another gets the shade."

CHINESE PROVERB

"My mother had a great deal of trouble with me, but I think she enjoyed it."

MARK TWAIN
(1835–1910)

"Your mother will always be the one person who tells you, 'Yes, you can'."

ANONYMOUS

"Our girls are the center of Barack's and my world. They're the reason he ran for President—to make the world a better place for them and for all children."

MICHELLE OBAMA (1964–)

Acknowledgments

The publishers are grateful for permission to reproduce extracts from works in copyright.

Page 50: Reprinted by kind permission of the OSHO International Foundation.

Page 51: From *Wilma Rudolph: Champion Athlete* by Tom Biracree (Holloway House Publishing, 1990)

Page 52: From *Young India*, 19 November 1931, page 361. Reprinted by kind permission of the Navajivan Trust.

Page 54: GreenLight, LLC and its affiliates represent publicity, trademark, and related rights of Mae West, on behalf of the Mae West Receivership. "Mae West" is a trademark of the Mae West Receivership.

Every effort has been made to contact copyright holders and acknowledge sources, but the publishers would be glad to hear of any omissions.

The editor would like to thank David Dean, esq., The Wicks and Whitney Ladies' Advice Service, Ms Carmel Edmonds, Mrs Pauline Hurley, PAH, ARH, CARH, MH, Fred H, Flora H, DJT, AP and Chef Giuliano Pertusini.

Index of authors